In 1979 Dr. John Newton preached at Raithby at a service which was held to mark the two hundredth anniversary of the opening by John Wesley of Raithby Chapel - built by Robert Carr Brackenbury, and now the oldest Methodist Chapel in Lincolnshire, and one of the oldest in the world.

It seemed to me that an annual lecture to commemorate the life and work of Robert Carr Brackenbury would draw attention to the existence and financial needs of this unique building, and I am grateful to the Society for Lincolnshire History and Archaeology, The Lincolnshire Methodist History Society, The Tennyson Society and the Spilsby Methodist Circuit who agreed to sponsor and advertise such an event each year.

Charles Brackenbury has been an enthusiastic supporter of the lectures since their inception, and it gave pleasure to all concerned when it was known that he was willing to lecture on the Brackenbury family in 1983. It gave equal pleasure to see a considerable number of members of the Brackenbury family present at the lecture - and there can be no doubt that there were more Brackenburys in Raithby on July 2nd 1983 than at any time since the death of Robert Carr Brackenbury in 1818.

With characteristic generosity Charles Brackenbury has donated the proceeds of the sale of the lecture to Raithby Chapel and the Society for Lincolnshire History and Archaeology.

Terence R. Leach,
Chairman
Local History Sub-Committee
Society for Lincolnshire
History and Archaeology

ISBN 0 904680 21 5

The Society for Lincolnshire
History & Archaeology,
47 Newland, Lincoln.
1983.

1. INTRODUCTION

1.   My aim this afternoon is to sketch the portrait of a Lincolnshire family which, without ever being very distinguished in British history, yet has held a fairly prominent position in Lincolnshire at one time or another.

2.   I have found, as so many researchers before me must have found, that facts resemble nothing so much as the croquet hoops in "Alice in Wonderland"; no sooner do you think you have them fixed than they get up and walk away. If any members of my audience know that anything I have stated as a fact is incorrect, I hope that, in the discussion at the end of my talk, they will tell me.

3.   There are four Brackenburys of the Lincolnshire family in the Dictionary of National Biography. Three were soldiers - Sir Edward of Skendleby, Sir Henry and his brother, Charles Booth Brackenbury. The fourth was Joseph, a clergyman and poet. Curiously enough, Robert Carr Brackenbury, who was perhaps the most distinguished member of the family, does not appear, although many other important Methodists do. Of these four I shall speak when they fit into their chronological places.

4.   There is one Brackenbury whose name is to be found in every history book - Sir Robert Brackenbury, who was Constable of the Tower of London and in charge of the Mint in the reign of Richard III. His reputation has suffered unjustly from the Tudor propaganda against Richard III, which had as little regard for the truth as Soviet propaganda today. Caroline Halstead, writing in 1848, says of him:

> *"He (Richard III) distinguished Brackenbury with marks of the highest favour, and there is no existing document or even tradition to prove him undeserving of the Prince's regard. With firmness and fidelity Brackenbury followed Gloucester's fortunes to the very close of his life, even at the sacrifice of his own".* [1]

5.   Sir Robert Brackenbury does not belong to the Lincolnshire family, but was a younger son of Thomas Brackenbury of Denton and Selaby, Co. Durham, the latter of which he inherited. The Brackenburys are traceable in Co. Durham from the end of the 12th century. There are references to Brackenburys in Lincolnshire from about fifty years earlier, who were quite clearly above the yeoman class. I believe there must have been a connection between these two families, if only one could find evidence of it.

II.   BRACKENBURYS LIVING IN LINCOLNSHIRE BEFORE 1500

1.   Brackenborough is a village 2½ miles north of Louth; it is mentioned in Domesday Book, and traces of a large Saxon village can be seen in aerial photographs. It is here that we first find people calling themselves Brakenburgh, or Brackenbury. It is probable that they took their name from the locality. Radulph de Brackenbury witnessed grants of land to houses of the Gilbertine Order in Ormsby and Alvingham in 1155, 1160 and 1166; in 1189 and 1199 he and a Thomas Brackenbury both acted as witnesses. The Gilbertine Order was the only indigenous English monastic Order and was almost unique in having both canons and nuns in

---

(1) *"The Crown and the Tower" - the Legend of Richard III:*
     William H. Snyder (ed.) pub. Richard III Society Inc. 1981

1

most of its houses. It was established in the mid-twelfth century by St. Gilbert in Sempringham, and other foundations quickly followed.

2. In 1200, Jordanus de Brackenbury witnessed deeds of gift to Ormsby and in 1202 he served on a jury at Lincoln Assizes. In the first half of the thirteenth century, Brackenburys were associated with the de Nevil family and with the Lords of Bayeux, who were the most powerful magnates in the area. In 1212, Jordanus de Brackenbury was buying land from Hugo of Bayeux in Kelstern (value Ł10.) In 1227, he was constituted justiciary in Lincoln.

3. In 1239 and 1245, Ranulph de Brackenbury witnessed two grants of land to Lincoln Cathedral. Ranulph was stated to be "Miles", that is Knight. Brackenburys had been acting for the Lords of Bayeux in many transactions and in 1288, a Robert de Brackenbury married Joan, who was the daughter of Elias de Rabayn and Matilda, daughter of Stephan of Bayeux. They appear to have been given the manor of Kelstern in fee tail by her father. After their deaths, their son Sir John entered into possession, but omitted to get the licence of the king from whom the manor was held in chief. Upon paying a fine of Ł10, the trespass was pardoned and the manor again granted to the Brackenburys. By now, the Brackenburys were themselves making grants of land to Louth Park Abbey. The land was in Brackenburgh and Duchenges.

4. There was a John Brackenbury of Housoum in Lincolnshire who, in 1347, was made Troner of Wool (i.e. the official who weighed the wool) in Hull. I think this was the John who was murdered at Michaelmas in 1360 by Robert de Manby of Worlikby (i.e. Worlaby). The murderer received a pardon in 1362 in view of his good service in the war with France. He was also relieved of outlawry suffered in consequence of the killing. This was the second Brackenbury to be murdered. Earlier in the century, William de Brackenbury had met a violent death at the hands of William Store, who was given a general pardon for his act in 1327. It was this William de Brackenbury who in 1294 witnessed, with his brother Gilbert, a charter giving lands in Sutton, "quit of all secular service save the prayers of poor men".

5. In 1349, Thomas de Brackenbury of the Order of the Friars Minor was appointed by the Pope to be Bishop of Leighlin in Ireland, south of Dublin. There appear to have been words prejudicial to the king and crown in the Bull appointing him, because it was only after he had given his fealty to the king expressly renouncing the offending remarks in the Bull, that the king issued a mandate to the justiciary of Ireland for the livery of the temporalities of the See to Thomas.

6. In 1349, too, the Black Death came to Lincolnshire, which suffered more than any other county and Brackenburgh was very badly hit. We know that after the Black Death, villages were often moved to new sites which is why the churches are often some distance from the present villages, the church being too solidly built to be moved with the village. Brackenburgh was surrounded by marsh and I suspect it was temporarily abandoned after the Black Death, the survivors moving to Alvingham and elsewhere. One family of Brackenburys moved to Thimbleby, where possibly they had land. A hundred years later, they were sufficiently important for William, who was buried in January 1476, to have a tombstone with brasses of himself, his wife Emotta and ten children.

2

7.   There are also references elsewhere to what we would call "strays". There was a London merchant, Thomas de Brackenbury, who in 1350 acknowledged a debt of ₤200 to Simon de Swanlond, Knight; it was cancelled on repayment. In 1352, he owed ₤136.5.0 to Henry, Duke of Lancaster, also cancelled on repayment. In the same year, a Thomas de Brackenbury married Beatrix de Swanlond. There is also a record that a Thomas de Brackenbury and his wife Joan obtained, in 1354, indults to choose their confessors. It is possible, of course, that Beatrix died within two years of marriage, and the widower then married Joan, but it is not necessarily true that either of these two Thomases was the London merchant. I think the London merchant was probably the Thomas de Brackenbury who came to Harefield in Middlesex in 1356 and owned a house there which is still called Brackenbury House. He built a chapel in Harefield Church known as the Brackenbury Chapel, but it was swept away when the church was restored in Victorian times.

8.   In 1487 died Sir John Brackenbury who wished to be buried before St. Paul's Cross. As he left money to the church in Hendon and named executors who were of Westminster and Fleet Street, he presumably lived in London. He had received land, tenements and messuages from William Brackenbury, which his mother was to have if she did not re-marry. This she had promised before the parson and parish of Thimbleby. The William from whom John inherited was probably the William Brackenbury to whom I have already referred who was buried in Thimbleby in January 1476.

9.   In 1497, a Richard Brackenbury died. He was Dean of the Collegiate Church of the Blessed Mary in Warwick. [2]
He left his best silver gilt flask and his best silver gilt salt cellar to make a chrismatory to the value of ₤20. He also left a silver gilt salt cellar, set with two chalcedonies, and a hundred sheep, to the church. He made several other bequests, including 20 shillings to each of his servants and 6/8 to "the boy Henry". He was evidently a man of substance. One of his executors was Thomas Brackenbury, who is designated "Magister" in the Latin text.

10.   Richard Brackenbury, sometimes called "the Courtier", who was one of the gentleman ushers to Queen Elizabeth, was not a Lincolnshire Brackenbury. He was the fifth son of Arthur Brackenbury of Selaby, Co. Durham. It has been said that he owned Skendleby, but I have been unable to verify this. I think it is doubtful.

11.   From 1540 on, we have a family tree continuing to the present day.

III.   THE ANCESTORS OF THE PRESENT BRACKENBURY FAMILY OF LINCOLNSHIRE

1.   I am now the head of the family of Brackenbury of Lincolnshire. I can trace my ancestry back to Thomas Brackenbury of Belchford who died in 1540. I think the family may have come to Belchford after the Black death.

(2) *Harleian MS 433 (p.280, Vol.1). "Maister Richard Brykburgh hath the denery of the Collegiate Church of Warwick by the resignation of Maister Albone"*

2.   The Brackenburys seem to have been moderately big fish in the very small pond of Belchford. Thomas was a juror of the Court of the Manor of Belchford from 1509 to 1513. In his will, which was proved at Lincoln in 1540, he left several legacies. His son Edward was also a juror of the Manor of Belchford. In his will, he disposed of a house and 18 acres or more of land which he had bought of Lord Willoughby; another house in which he lived, with 36 acres; yet another house and 36 acres of which he held copyhold of the Queen, and many small legacies. His will was proved at Horncastle in 1558.

3.   The Bishop's transcripts for Belchford start in 1561. A Brackenbury was then churchwarden. Between 1561 and 1666 there were many baptisms of Brackenburys recorded, and many deaths, but curiously enough comparatively few marriages.

4.   Frances Brackenbury who died a widow in 1633 left a house comprising solar, chamber, hall, buttery, dairy, barn and yard. She was survived by two sons and one daughter.

5.   Miles Brackenbury, who died in 1610, called himself a husbandman. His son Miles was a miller and his grandson, also Miles, called himself a yeoman. He died in 1645 at Baumber. By now, they have gone up in the world. Miles of Baumber left copyhold in Orby, plus Ł40 and freehold land in Orby plus Ł40 – the Ł40 were to be for the education of his two elder sons, both under 21. His youngest son and his daughter were each to receive Ł60 when they came of age. After several small legacies, he left the rest of his goods to his wife Hester.

6.   What is, or more specifically what was, a gentleman? In the fifteenth century, the use of the terms "gentleman" and "yeoman" became obligatory in court pleas, after the Statute of Additions in 1413. However this does not seem to have led to precise definitions. Technically, a gentleman is one who is not noble but is entitled to bear arms. Clive Holmes, in his very interesting "Seventeenth Century Lincolnshire", suggests that the term was ambiguous and elastic at that time. The coveted suffix "Gentleman" was accorded to, and more frequently claimed by, men who were in other respects indistinguishable from the better class of farmer, tradesman or professional man.

7.   This question is relevant because Miles, who died in 1645, called himself a yeoman, while his son Thomas, in his will dated 1702, called himself a gentleman, and sealed his will with coat-of-arms and crest, to which he does not seem to have been entitled. Thomas's brother William, in his will, called himself a yeoman; his brother Richard, who died unmarried, a bachelor.

8.   It is interesting that the Bishop's Transcripts for Belchford from the beginning in 1561 until 1666 contain many items concerning Brackenburys but that after 1666 there are no further references except one christening in 1782, of Robert, son of Robert and Mary. [3]   Presumably the family had moved away. The first entry in the Bishop's Transcripts for Steeping Magna which refers to the family is dated 1667, the baptism of a son of Thomas's brother William, who lived in Monkthorpe.

(3) *Mormon Records*

9.   Thomas, son of Miles of Baumber, was born in 1637 and lived at Great Steeping. He became an attorney, beginning the family's connection with the law. He married, first, Ann, whose maiden name is not known. They had four sons and one daughter. As his second wife he married Elizabeth Boddington, the widow of Charles Rogers. She is said to have come of a rich London merchant family, trading to the East Indies. They had one son and three daughters.

10.   Unfortunately, very little is known of Thomas and his two wives. It would be extremely interesting to know who Ann's family were, and also rather more about Elizabeth's family, Boddington, and her first husband Charles Rogers.

11.   This is the moment to take stock. We have seen that there were in the 13th and 14th century Brackenburys living in Brackenborough and Louth where they were closely connected with Louth Park Abbey. They were knights and landowners. The fact that we can find no trace of the family in the records after 1349 means little. The more simple annals of parish registers, Bishop's Transcripts, etc. are not available. As we have seen, between 1350 and 1540, there are records of Brackenburys with Lincolnshire connections who were living elsewhere and references to Brackenburys living in Thimbleby. In a deed of enfoeffment dated 1611 in the parish records of Alvingham, the next village to Brackenborough, there is mention of a messuage and tenement lately in the tenure of Thomas Brackenbury.

12.   Family fortunes often disappear in the course of a few years. It is not unreasonable therefore to suppose that the Brackebburys who died in Belchford in the 1540s were descended from those earlier Brackenburys who lived under 10 miles away, and vanished from the records at the time of the Black Death. We do not know how long before 1540 there were Brackenburys in Belchford. In 1531, Thomas Vynsaynt of Belchford left 4 pence in his will to the wife of Robert Brackenbury and to every godchild. This is the only connection with Belchford that I have found before parish records started in the sixteenth century.

13.   From Thomas who died at Great Steeping in 1702 and called himself "Gentleman", the descent is clear and we know much more about the activities of the members of the family.

14.   Thomas's brother William of Monkthorpe begat a line which continues to this day. Among its more distinguished members were Sir Henry Britten Brackenbury, who was Chairman of the Council of the British Medical Association and its Vice-president in the 1930s, Sir Cecil Fabian Brackenbury, who had a distinguished career in the Indian Civil Service, and his son John, who was Warden of the Impington Village College and retired a few years ago.

IV.   THOMAS OF STEEPING MAGNA AND HIS DESCENDANTS

1.   Thomas died and was buried in Great Steeping in 1702. In 1690 he had been admitted to Clement's Inn. There was a monument to him at Steeping on which it was stated that he had married twice. Unfortunately, this monument has disappeared or we might have learnt more from it. Although Thomas, in his will, described himself as "Gent." and signed

with a coat-of-arms and crest, his will gives the impression of being that of a yeoman, particularly when compared to that of his son. As he left by his will small legacies to the children of his first wife and all his free-hold lands in Great Steeping to his widow (i.e. his second wife), with remainder to her son Carr, it may be assumed that she was the heiress who brought this land with her on her marriage. (Among other legacies she left on her death a gold watch to her granddaughter.)

2.   Thomas, eldest son of the previous Thomas by his first wife, married Elizabeth, daughter of his father's second wife by her first husband. They married in 1694 and had two daughters but no son. One daughter, Isabella, married William Booth of Ashby Puerorum and Aswardby. Their daughter, also Isabella, married Carr Brackenbury, the son of the first Carr, i.e. she married her first cousin once removed.

3.   However, interest centres for us on Thomas's brother Carr, born in 1688 and died in 1741. He married first, in 1710, Ann, daughter of Langley Gace of Panton and Hardwicke. She died in 1727.

4.   Three years after the death of his wife Anne Gace, Carr the first married Ann, daughter of Sir John Tyrwhitt, baronet, of Stainfield. She was in debt at the time of the marriage, and Carr spent ₤200 to satisfy various creditors. As at the time of Carr's death in 1741, the marriage portion of ₤6,000 had not yet been paid although 11 years had passed, we may assume that Sir John Tyrwhitt was hard up, The marriage portion was to be used to discharge a mortgate of ₤6,000 on Carr's Lusby property to the Trustees of the Duke of Ancaster.

5.   Ann Tyrwhitt bore four children, one stillborn, two who died within a few months of their birth and one son, James, who survived. She died in 1787, fifty-seven years after she had married Carr, so she must have been of a considerable age, even if she was quite young when she married with debts of ₤200. She was living in Lincoln when she made her will in 1783, which was proved in 1788. She left ₤10 to a Mrs. Clark "my late son's widow". This must have been the widow of James. One item in her will speaks volumes as to her character. She says "And whereas the family of the Brackenburys have not thought it worth their while to pay me any friendly attention supposing as I apprehend that I had nothing to give them And whereas my sister Waddington nor her daughter have thought proper to answer my letters, tho' I have wrote to her several times, I do hereby give all the rest of my goods . . . . to my good friend Jephtha Foster Gentleman". She must have been a difficult woman. Did Carr regret his second marriage? He does call her his loving wife in his will but that sounds conventional, and the tone of the will when it refers to the marriage portion and the debts is stern.

6.   Carr was admitted to Clement's Inn in 1714; the next year he bought a lease of his chambers for his life and for an assignment for one other life after the expiration of his own. For this he paid ₤130. He may also have been an estate accountant, and was certainly Clerk of the Sewers, because I have seen his signature as such on minutes of a meeting on 1 October 1725. He was sufficiently successful to be appointed Receiver General for Lincolnshire in 1741, when he was 53 years old. He died in November of the same year. His will shows him to have been a very wealthy man. He owned land in forty-three areas in Lindsey, as well as land in Boston and Skirbeck. He left his chambers in Clement's Inn to

his son Thomas, together with his farms in Hertfordshire, and Thomas was duly admitted to Clement's Inn in 1742. There seems to have been a close connection between Clement's Inn and Lincolnshire. Between 1659 and 1742, 49 Lincolnshire men were admitted. Carr wished to be buried at Spilsby or in the chancel at Lusby - he held the advowson of Lusby and he and Ann Tyrwhitt had been married there.

7.   It is interesting that he owned nothing in Stainfield, nor is his only child by his second wife, James, mentioned in the will except for part of the ₺300 jointure left to his widow and as the last, after all the sons by his first wife, in the reversion of the entail male of the large portion of his estate settled on his eldest son Carr.

8.   It is in 1688 that the name Carr appears in the family for the first time. The rise to great wealth of the first Carr would account for the use of the name in future generations, but it is not known why Thomas and Elizabeth called their first (and only) son Carr. It was to the Dukes of Ancaster that the family mainly owed its rise. Maybe Elizabeth Boddington's mother was a Carr of Sleaford, although there does not seem to be a suitable candidate in the Carr family tree. Possibly Carr's godfather was a Carr of Sleaford and put the family on the road to success by introducing them to the Dukes of Ancaster.

9.   I am now faced with a problem. When Dr. Tennyson, the Poet Laureate's father, wished to curse the Brackenbury family for taking the rooms he wanted in Mablethorpe, he referred to the "race of Brackenburys", and not to the "family". It was also said that at the balls in Spilsby in the nineteenth century, one could count a hundred Brackenburys. To do justice to all members and all branches of the family I would have to go on all day and most of tomorrow. Already, in one paragraph, I have shed a large and flourishing branch of the family who, even though they now rate as a Cambridgeshire family, are of our Lincolnshire stock and have many interesting members.

10.   By his first wife, the first Carr had six sons and one daughter who survived childhood, and one son by his second wife. I propose to follow the fortunes of the senior branch through Carr the second, but before doing so, will make brief reference to some of the other branches.

11.   At the beginning of the eighteenth century, Brackenburys were going into the law as country solicitors and into the Church for the first time. At this time, no Brackenburys were entering the medical profession, though one Brackenbury daughter married a surgeon of Spilsby in 1759.

12.   Carr the first's second son, Joseph, married Elizabeth Leach and was the progenitor of a large and important family; included among his descendants are Henry Langton Brackenbury who was MP for the Louth or East Lindsey division of Lincolnshire from 1910 to 1920, and Robin Brackenbury, who was High Sheriff of Nottingham last year. Joseph took Holy Orders and was presented to the living of Holton Holgate by the Duke of Ancaster. His eldest son Joseph became a lawyer, and founded a firm whose portfolio included clerkship of the Lindsey Court of Sewers, mainly responsible for the drainage of the coastal marshlands in the nineteenth century. Also among the descendants of Joseph and Elizabeth (Leach) was the poet Joseph, who found his way into the Dictionary of

National Biography. His published verse was rather pedestrian, but his unpublished verse was much more fun. He was chaplain to the Magdalene Hospital in Blackfriars.

13.   The third son, Thomas Carr, married Elizabeth Ostler of Scremby. He inherited his father's chambers in Clement's Inn and carried on the legal business there. As well as being an attorney-at-law, he was a land agent. He was Clerk of the Sewers and for some years Clerk of the Peace. He was appointed the first Treasurer to the Whole of the Parts of Lindsey, and held office from 1750 until his death in 1771. His son Charles bought Scremby Hall which was one of the largest units of land owned by the Brackenbury family - rather more than 1,000 acres, which was large for an estate in the Wolds.

14.   Among Charles's sons was Henry, who became rector of Scremby. He married Anne Atkinson who was a particularly close friend of the poet Tennyson's sister Mary, who wrote: "Gloriana", as she called her, "is so sweet a character and she has always been so kind and so anxious for our family. I look upon her as already a saint". Henry kept a pack of harriers at Scremby, which he converted in 1820 into foxhounds. They were first called the Gillingham, but in 1823 became the South Wold. Joseph Brackenbury hunted them in 1827 and 1829, and of course the late Diana Brackenbury was Joint Master from 1930 to 1945.

15.   Another of Charles's sons, Augustus, was an interesting character. In 1820, at the age of 28, he went off to Wales where he bought land near Aberystwith under the Government enclosure scheme. No doubt he thought of enclosure as an operation which benefited all parties as it had done in Lincolnshire. The Welsh thought otherwise and burned him out. He went to live in London where he developed a method of preparing common salt which he claimed was far more economical than the process then in use. In 1849, he issued a circular setting out the benefits. He needed only £50 to develop the process and foresaw an annual profit of £34,000. As far as I know, nothing came of the project. Augustus died unmarried in 1874. His venture in Wales was the subject of a poem commissioned from Jeremy Hooker by the BBC and the Welsh Art Council and broadcast in 1979.

16.   The fourth son of the first Carr was Langley Gace Brackenbury, who went off to become a brewer in Epsom. At a slightly later date, George Meredith made the point in "Evan Harrington" that the profession of brewer was socially acceptable, while that of tailor was not. The sixth son, John, never married. He dropped down dead at the front door of his brother's house in Epsom on 4 November 1779, in his fifties. He was buried at Spilsby.

17.   To return to Carr the second, eldest son of the first Carr. He appears to have been a somewhat feckless or scatterbrained man. He was sole executor of his father's will, which he proved in the Prerogative Court of Canterbury on 3 December 1741. On his death in 1763, the administration of the will was not complete. In July 1804, Edward Bray of Great Russell Street was appointed to wind it up.

18.   Carr was born in 1714. From the portrait which I had of him, he was a handsome man, perhaps rather heavily built. In a later portrait, he has thickened considerably, but is still impressive. In 1742, he married his cousin, grand-daughter of his uncle Thomas of

Spilsby, Isabella Booth. They were married in St. Margaret's, Westminster. She was an heiress and is said to have had Ŀ1,500 a year and Ŀ40,000. In the same year Carr bought Panton Hall from his first cousin Gace, and he and his wife went to live there.

ANNEX II

19.   I do not have time to discuss the vagaries of Carr's will. Suffice it to say that, in his will, Carr directed that Panton should be sold. He had ten children but only the first six had been born when he made his will in 1757 and benefited under it. The six elder children were Robert Carr, Edward and four daughters; the four younger were William, Richard, Langley and Charlotte, who were to have benefited under a codicil made in 1762. When the claims of the first six under the will had been satisfied, there was nothing left for the younger four.

ANNEX III

20.   Carr's eldest son was Robert Carr, who is probably the best known member of the Lincolnshire family, particularly in Methodist circles. Even though it is to remember him that we are here today, I shall give only a brief outline of his life. Perhaps Terence Leach, who knows so much about him, will consider devoting one of these lectures in the near future entirely to him and his labours for Methodism.

21.   Robert Carr was born in 1752 at Panton and died at Raithby in 1818. He was educated at Felstead and St. Catherine's College, Cambridge. In an obituary, it was stated that he had been well-known on the Turf. This has always been dismissed as incorrect, but it has struck me that he might, like so many wealthy undergraduates, have followed horse-racing in his youth. He would then join a distinguished company who suffered a revulsion from the sowing of wild oats for, while at Cambridge, he seems to have had an intense religious experience which seriously affected his health. By his twenty-fourth year, he had been introduced to Methodism and had abandoned his previous intention of entering the Church. In 1776, he met Wesley and became one of his closest friends. Wesley was then 73 years old. Before Robert Carr was thirty, he had built Raithby; he had already built the chapel where we are now, and which Wesley dedicated when he visited Robert Carr in July 1779. At that date, only the shell of the house was finished.

22.   The surname of Robert Carr's first wife, Jane, is not known. I have the impression that she was a charming person - certainly Wesley had a high opinion of her. She died at the age of 21 as the result of an accident. Her foot slipped as she was entering her carriage, causing severe internal injury from which she died after several months of illness. One cannot help asking "Was she pregnant at the time?" Robert Carr married again in 1795, his second wife being Sarah Holland of Loughborough, whom he met when they were both visiting a sick friend. They had no children. Even though Sarah has been called "a most excellent Christian woman" [4]   I cannot like her; she seems to me to have been ungenerous, though deeply religious. It may well be that she was aware of opposition to her on the part of the Brackenbury family, and she certainly managed to keep Robert Carr's heirs out of their inheritance by living until 1847. Though enormously wealthy, she appears never to have helped her husband's family, but rather to have exploited the properties in which she had a life interest so that they were worth very little at her death.

(4) *Endorsed at the top of her letter of 27 July 1834 to James Montgomery*

Though willing to spend large sums on Methodist missions and even on making good Methodists out of South Sea Islanders, she appears to have done nothing for her brother-in-law, Langley, who was living in poverty and great distress. It was to him that Robert Carr left Raithby, subject to his wife's life interest. One would have expected her to have felt some responsibility in the matter. What ultimately happened to Robert Carr's great estate I do not know.

23.   I have read many of Sarah's letters and much of her diary. Apart from references to her late husband, I have come across only one reference to his family. It is dated August 1834 and refers to Sir Edward, her husband's nephew, then still a Major:- "In a fortnight after the Major had lost his wife, his youngest little boy died of water on the brain. Surely such afflications are intended to answer some great end - and should they bring the Major to that Saviour who is seldom found in the moments of prosperity, his loss will be his richest gain". Not exactly an expression of sympathy.

24.   Robert Carr was the eldest of six brothers, one of whom, George, died in infancy. When Robert Carr was 11 and his youngest brother Langley was 4, their father died. Their mother married again, and the family moved to Essex. Panton was sold in accordance with the directions in his father's will. All the brothers except Langley later returned to Lincolnshire and made their homes there.

25.   It is interesting to compare the situation of the brothers as young men, that is to say, the effect of their father's will on their fortunes. Robert Carr as a young man in his twenties was sufficiently wealthy to build himself a country house in a fine estate characterized by Wesley as an earthly paradise. The second brother George having died, the third brother Edward seems to have been provided for under his father's will and to have inherited Skendleby. The fourth brother William settled in Grimsby. I know nothing about him except that he married twice and had one daugher by his second wife. He was the eldest of the four children not provided for under his father's will. As I have said, after the six eldest children had received their portion, there was nothing left for the four for whom it had been intended to make provision under a codicil. The fifth brother, Richard, became a soldier at the age of 18. He had to borrow from his uncle Langton £200 with which to purchase his ensign's commission in the 70th Regiment of Foot and pay bills and travelling expenses to Edinburgh, where the regiment was stationed. He undertook to repay the loan with lawful interest on attaining the age of 21. It was repaid after his mother's death in 1780 when he was 22. His uncle Langton did not claim interest.

26.   There seems to have been a stern, not to say mean, strain in Robert Carr. Why did Richard have to borrow from his uncle when his brother was so wealthy? Perhaps Robert Carr was anti-military and did not approve of Richard's becoming a soldier. Robert Carr also seems to have neglected his youngest brother Langley who, as we shall see, was in financial distress in the 1790s. One gets the impression that Langley had behaved in some way that Robert Carr must have disapproved of.

27.   Langley seems to have been a born loser. He never returned to Lincolnshire to live. I have a letter from him to his brother Edward written in London on 20 April 1797 - that is when he was 38 - to "express my surprise at your writing to me for money who has been a beggar the past seven years and God only knows when I shall be anything else". He goes on to say: "As my relations think proper to keep me poor as any beggar

in the capacity of a servant which I never meritted any more than any one of them, I have thought proper to take unto me a wife". In 1818, a few months before his death, Robert Carr borrowed Ł500 of a Miss Hicks of Leicester to lend to Langley. In a codicil to his will, he made stern provisions that whatever arrangements might be made to repay Miss Hicks, Langley should ultimately be responsible, even to the extent of with-holding the annuity of Ł200 left to Langley in his will, until such time as the Ł500 plus interest was repaid. Furthermore, in 1821, Langley drew a bill of exchange on Edward which the latter accepted. This was possibly to satisfy Robert Carr's estate for the repayment of Robert Carr's borrowing from Miss Hicks. It came home to roost a year later, when the Reigate Bank presented it to Edward for payment. By now, Langley had other worries. His son Robert was very ill. In a letter from Brighton dated 25 March 1822, he writes of the indisposition of Robert, who had a hard swelling in the lower part of his groin, which had discharged freely after being lanced. The doctor perceived that there was great danger in the situation. Langley ends: "Please write soon as I am afraid from appearances that I shall have to announce the worst". I can find no record of Robert's burial in Brighton. At Edward's death in 1828, a bill for Ł500 was due by Langley to him, but Edward stipulated in his will that it should not be called until after Sarah's death, when Langley was to inherit Raithby.

28.   We know little enough about Langley. He was born in 1759 and died at Hurstpierpoint in Sussex in July 1832 aged 74 years. He had married in 1797 when he was 38. His wife's name was Elizabeth; she died at Brighton in 1824 aged 54. He had at least nine children, possibly more; eight were born at Rusper in Sussex, and Robert, who was so ill in 1822, was born elsewhere. There were two sons born at Rusper – Langley Carr in 1800, and William in 1810. Langley Carr may have been the Langley who married Rebecca Lee at Old Charlton in Kent in 1827. We know he died before his father, in Hurstpierpoint in May 1832. I suspect he was the eldest son.

29.   A speculation – Langley named his sons, Langley Carr, William, Robert – all family names of himself and his brothers. May he not also have had a son Richard? There was a Richard Brackenbury who married a Margaret Reilly at St. George's, Hanover Square on 17 April 1837. The witnesses were John Geo. Leigh, a vestry clerk and Sara Reaks, who had to make her mark, because she could not write. The curate officiated.

30.   Edward, the second son of Carr the second, became a clergyman and was Vicar of Skendleby and also of Aswardby. He was Justice of the Peace. He lived at Skendleby, which he owned. His wife was Mary Joyce, eighth daughter of William Massingbird of Gunby. As the Massingbirds were always in financial difficulties, her dowry cannot have been large. I think it is time to defend Edward's reputation from the accusation that he was "grasping" – an accusation enshrined in the LAO Reports and repeated by Terence Leach. The basis of this charge is that he lent the Massingbirds money at 7% when, as the LAO Report says, loans were available at 3½%. But were they? If the Massingbirds could obtain loans at 3½%, why did they pay 7%? The answer is that they had already raised all the money at lower interest rates that they could lay their hands on. Edward must have seen no end to the Massingbird's need for money. As no one is likely to have considerable sums lying idle, he would have had to borrow at 3½%. He no doubt saw no reason why he should not have interest on his loan, particularly as it must have looked

like a bad debt. The Massingbirds seem to have thought him mean because he would not lend them more, but this is frequently the attitude of congenital borrowers. I have a most friendly letter from Peregrine Massingbird, written on 2 August 1819 to Edward from near Bordeaux. It sets out his plans for economy. He says: "I would to God that sooner I had taken your advice, and from the beginning of 17 years past had followed your example". He says that even before receiving Edward's last letter he had set in train certain economies which he details. After referring to the marriage of Lord Buckinghamshire, who was the tenant of Gunby, he says: "I am sorry you do not visit there, and more so as occasionally to have taken a round there of the plantations would have been a great kindness towards me and an encouragement to Parker (Peregrine's agent)". The whole tone of the letter belies the remark attributed to him that Edward "was one of the proudest, vulgarest-minded men I was ever acquainted with". It is interesting that Algernon, Peregrine's son, was able to rescue the Gunby estate as soon as he took charge on his coming of age in 1825; his father presumably could have done so if he had not been incurably extravagant.

31.   Edward also did all he could to rescue the Brackenbury inheritance from the depredations of Sarah and her Holland relations. He protested to Sarah that, without informing him, she had offered Langley ₤10,000 for the reversion of Raithby and had endeavoured to purchase the two principal farms of his brother William in Lusby. She provoked Edward by asking him "on the grounds of mutual courtesy" to let her have the offer of his reversionary interest in Donington-on-Bain, should he feel disposed to part with it. He countered by proposing to buy out her life interest. To this she replied that her "friend" - whom I suppose to be her brother - had advised her that it would not be in her interest to do so, although the terms she mentioned were ₤10,000 plus ₤600 per annum for the rest of her life. No doubt Edward, fighting a costly battle to save the Brackenbury inheritance, was unwilling to do much for that of the Massingbirds.

32.   Edward's widow, who died in 1839 aged 70, had founded a school in Lincoln when she was living there as a widow in the Close with her sister. According to the "Gentleman's Magazine", "her ample fortune was expended in the exercise of unbounding benevolence". The bulk of her property, which she must have had from her husband, devolved on Sir Edward Brackenbury, who also inherited Skendleby from the Rev. Edward, his uncle.

33.   The fifth son of Carr was Richard who lived at Aswardby and was the only one of the brothers, with the possible exception of Langley, to leave sons living at his death. From his portrait, he seems to have had a mischievous sense of humour. He was born in 1758 and died in 1844. He married, at the age of 18, Janetta, daughter of George Gunn of Edinburgh. She brought him little fortune so they must have been hard up in the first years of their marriage. His uncle John regarded Richard's marriage as an indiscretion but nevertheless sent him ₤20 and the following advice "worthy of the attention of all young married couples - to please and be pleased, to bear and forbear, to wink and forgive".

34.   Richard did not stay long in the Army. He returned to Lincolnshire. He lived partly at Robert Carr's house, Raithby, and partly at Aswardby. Aswardby had come to Robert Carr from his mother and he left it to his brother when he died in 1818, but Richard appears to have

been living there before that, because, in 1813, his son William wrote him a rather pathetic letter in which he refers to returning home to Aswardby. I shall refer to this letter later in its proper place. The rent roll of Aswardby, "this little property" was £373 in 1800; it was an estate of 570 acres.

35. Richard's finances are a mystery to me. He had to borrow from his uncle to buy his commission in 1776, and seems to have been poor in 1808 but when he died he was wealthy and owned a large collection of pictures, including a Gainsborough, a Cuyp, a Wouwerman, two Wilsons, two Breughels and many more.

36. Richard strongly disapproved of his brother Robert Carr becoming a Methodist, particularly a Methodist preacher. Richard had by then joined the Lincolnshire Militia and he sent his troops to parade outside the place where Robert Carr was preaching, and endeavoured to drown the sermon by the beating of drums. It is reported that his brother "in nothing terrified by any adversary" kept on his way, knowing whose he was and whom he served. Richard's attitude changed subsequently; he embraced Methodism and was himself a Class Leader and local preacher. He said he would have become a circuit preacher had it not been for his wife and children.

37. His wife died in 1827 when he was 68. By 1829, he was involved with, and proposed to marry, "a female from Bolingbroke" as his son William described her. No doubt with the example of Sarah still before them, his sons were very much opposed to the marriage. On 23 December 1829 Richard confessed to his son William that he contemplated a union with her as the only means of removing his sufferings and prolonging his life. After discussion with William his views seemed to change. "He firmly and manfully resolved never to take this step". Nevertheless, temptation was too strong for him. He slipped away and married her on 17 April 1830. She was Alice Horn of The Cottage, Bolingbroke, and was said to be a farmer's daughter. Richard's grandson, General Sir Henry Brackenbury, remembered her as a widow of immense proportions. She is buried in Aswardby Churchyard.

38. Alice's will, proved on 7 April 1868, suggests a kindly, if simple, soul. She left to Sir Henry Brackenbury the portrait of her husband, Richard, which had been given her by her step-son William, on condition that she left it by her will to William's son. She left to George, son of the Rev. Joseph Brackenbury, a silver coffee pot with arms and crest, two silver cups and two gravy spoons with the crest only, because he had been a friend to her. The remainder of her property she left to her sister's daughter.

39. Carr also had five daughters. Grace married without her guardian's consent when she was under age. Her property was thrown into Chancery, she receiving the income half-yearly. Her first marriage ended in divorce and she married William Marshall. Her son was Henry Cracroft Marshall.

40. Another daughter, Charlotte, married John Badely, M.D. of Chelmsford. He died aged 83 and was buried at Chelmsford by torchlight on Sunday, 21 July 1881. His widow survived him by eight years and died, also aged 83 years.

41.   So much for Carr's children. Richard of Aswardby had six sons and five daughters by his first wife Janetta. Two sons died early and one, Robert, entered the Navy. He was taken ill in St. Helena and was sent home, in a dying condition, on board the merchant ship "Cuffnells", in which he died on 16 July 1803, aged 20, and was buried at sea.

42.   The other three sons had distinguished careers. John Macpherson Brackenbury was born in 1778 and entered the 25th Light Dragoons; he appears to have been stationed at Winchester and Maidstone, where he was known to Lady Hester Stanhope. Her comment, in a letter, was not entirely flattering. "Griselda and Lucy will be at the troop tomorrow ... They will probably be accompanied by a smart young man, a Captain Brackenbury. Griselda danced with him at Sir Henry's fine ball. Though Captain Brackenbury is nothing extraordinary in himself yet he is quite wonderful for this neighbourhood".

43.   John Macpherson soon left the Army; when he was 22, he married Sophia Nichelson. He was appointed for three years to superintend the arrangements for saving the lives of shipwrecked sailors on the Lancashire coast. This was in connection with the life-saving rocket, invented by Sir William Congreve, who became a friend and after whom John Macpherson named his youngest son. According to Dixon, he contested the borough of Grimsby in the 1820 election but obtained only 31 votes. For some reason, three of his daughters and two of his sons were all baptised at Ilfracombe in Devon on 4 June 1810.

44.   He was appointed Consul in Cadiz where he remained happily for many years. Lord Beaconsfield in a letter to his father dated from Cadiz on 14 July 1830 wrote: "The English Consul here maintains a very elegant establishment, and has a very accomplished and amusing family. He prides himself on making all English of distinction dine with him every day. Fortunately his cook is ill, for being French and a very good one, I should have sunk under it. But Mrs. Brackenbury receives every evening and, whenever one is at a loss, it is agreeable to take refuge in a house which is literally a palace covered with pictures, where the daughters are all pretty and sing boleros." Disraeli thought John Macpherson "great enough for an ambassador", adding that he "lives well enough for one".

45.   George Borrow was in Cadiz in the summer of 1839. His account of John Macpherson and the Consulate is flattering:
"A few hours after my arrival, I waited upon Mr. Brackenbury, the British Consul General in Cadiz. I had of course long been acquainted with Mr. B. by reputation; I knew that for several years he had filled with advantage to his native country and with honour to himself, the distinguished and highly responsible situation which he holds in Spain. I saw him now for the first time and was much struck with his appearance. He is a tall, athletic, finely built man, seemingly about forty-five or fifty" - Actually, he was 61! - "There is much dignity in his countenance which is, however, softened by an expression of good humour, truly engaging. His manner is frank and affable in the extreme .. On the afternoon of Saturday, I dined with Mr. B. and his family - an interesting group - his lady, his beautiful daughters, and his son, a fine intelligent young man". Early next morning Borrow left by ship for Gibraltar. He adds: "I quitted this excellent man and my other charming friends, at a late hour with regret. In whatever part of the world, I, a poor wanderer in the Gospel's cause may chance to be, I shall not infrequently offer up sincere prayers for their happiness and well-being".

46.   John Macpherson was a great collector of pictures.   Indeed he was one of the three main British collectors of Spanish painting, who were all living in the south of Spain in 1830.   His collection included Murillo's portrait of Don Andrés de Andrade, which is now in the Metropolitan Museum in New York.   Richard Ford, the well-known writer and collector, was welcomed to Spain by John Macpherson on his first arrival.

47.   John Macpherson was Consul for 1822 - 1842.   On his retirement, he was made a knight bachelor and in 1845 a Knight of the Royal Guelphic Order of Hanover.   Curiously enough, he was Consul of His Majesty the King of Hanover in Cadiz and Consul for her Britannic Majesty for the Province of Andalusia.   On his return to England, he became a magistrate for the Parts of Lindsey.   He was referred to by other parts of the family as "that pompous old bore".

48.   He died in London in November 1847, so he never benefited from the legacy left him by his uncle Edward, who was to have received it from Robert Carr on Sarah's death, because he died only five months after Sarah.   It appears that the estate of Donington-on-Bain was in bad condition;   it was sold two months after his death.   His collection of pictures was also sold in London, in 1848.

49.   John Macpherson had three sons and six daughters.   William Congreve Cutliffe Brackenbury was the only son to have children. William married Magdalena Julia McGillivray of Montreal.   There is a charming portrait of him as a midshipman in the Royal Navy by the well-known Spanish artist Gutierez de la Vega.   On leaving the Navy, he joined the Consular Service;   he was Consul in Madrid, Bilbao, Vigo and Coruna, where he died and is buried.   He had two sons and two daughters.   The elder son, John William Brackenbury, joined the Navy; at the end of a distinguished career, he retired with the rank of Admiral;   the other son Maule went into the Army.   One of the daughters, Magdalena, married a Spaniard, Manuel Delgado y Zuleta.   She had six sons and we still have a very large and flourishing Spanish connection.

50.   Admiral John Brackenbury had three daughters.   Margaret, who married Lionel Colledge and Angela, who married Adrian Cornwell-Clyne; each had a son and a daughter.   Sadly, the two sons were killed in the last war;   the daughters are still living.   The second daughter, Olive, married Lt. Col. Philip Storey, DSO with bar;   they had no children.   Colonel Maule Brackenbury also had no children, so the descent of John Macpherson in the male line died out.

51.   Edward, fourth son of Richard of Aswardby, was born in 1784 at Raithby.   He married twice - firstly, Maria, daughter of the Rev. Edward Bromhead of Reepham.   They had two sons, both of whom died before coming of age.   He married secondly Eleanor, widow, of William Belford Clarke and daughter of Addison Fenwick.   She was the sister-in-law of R.S. Surtees, the creator of Mr. Jorrocks.   Surtees and Edward corresponded frequently because their wives were beneficiaries under a trust set up by their father which caused difficulties.   Edward and Eleanor had two sons;   the younger died aged 21, the elder survived to the age of 59;   he was my grandfather.

52.   Edward entered the Army and had a distinguished career in the Peninsular war, where he served first in the 61st Regiment and later commanded a Portuguese battalion under General Beresford. He ended his service as a Lt. Colonel, having sold out in 1847. He became Sir Edward in 1836. His army career is thus described in Hart's Annual Army List, 1859:

"Lt. Col. Sir Edward Brackenbury served in the 61st Regiment in Sicily, in Calabria, at Scylla Castle and at Gibraltar in 1807/8. In the Peninsula from 1809 to the end of that war in 1814, including the battles of Talavera and Busaco, Lines at Tores Vedras, pursuit of the French from Portugal, battle of Fuentes d'Onor, storming and capture of Badajoz – horse shot in advancing to the attack; battle of Salamanca – took a piece of artillery from the enemy guarded by four soldiers close to their retiring column, without any near or immediate support". This exploit was reported officially by his General of Brigade – "retreat from Burgos, action at Villa Muriel and Osuna (horse shot), battle of Vittoria; siege, two assaults and capture of San Sebastian, passage of the Bidassoa, battles of the Nivelle and the Nive, actions in front of Bayonne near the Mayor's house on the 10th, 11th and 12th Dec., (slightly wounded and horse shot); blockade of Bayonne and repulse of the sortie. Has received war medal with nine clasps; is Knight of the Order of St. Fernando of Spain; a Knight of the Tower and Sword, and a Commander of St. Benito d'Avis of Portugal". I wonder if an officer obtained replacements from the remount depot for horses shot under him, or whether he had to pay for them himself.

53.   There are various glimpses of Edward's life. There is a letter written in the field immediately after the Battle of Salamanca to which I shall refer later. I have a letter written to his wife, Maria, from London on 18 September 1827. He was concerned about his immediate future in the Army. He had seen Sir Herbert Taylor and Lord Fitzroy Somerset (later Lord Raglan of the Crimea) and was to attend a Levée of the Duke of Wellington. He was expecting to join the 56th Regiment. He ends this part of the letter: "You have married a soldier and you must share his fate. But this much I promise you that if we do not find it agreeable and I cannot get forward, I will retire again".

54.   He was friendly with that eccentric character Sir William Amcotts-Ingilby, who used to address him as the Duke of Braganza, starting his letter "Dear Duke" and finishing "Give my love to the Old Duchess". He said: "I know full well that with you (at Skendleby) I am in Casa Mia". One wonders how the rather serious-minded soldier enjoyed his company. I also have a letter from Augusta Cracroft, Sir William Amcotts-Ingilby's sister, dated tiresomely 27 August without the year, from Hackthorn. It was most probably written in 1832, for it refers to Edward's zealous and effective labours for the good cause during the 1832 election campaign, which her brother would always remember.

55.   In politics, Sir Edward was a Liberal in a predominantly Conservative area. When the North Lincolnshire Liberal Association was launched in 1853, he was looked to to organize the Spilsby district. There was little he could do in a district dominated by the Willoughby and Christopher Tory interests. In January 1855, Lord Monson wrote to urge him to take the lead in the Spilsby district but he replied that Liberal farmers and tradespeople did not care to risk giving offence by having their names published as members of a committee, particularly between elections.

56.   In Rashdall's diary on 27 November 1833 - Rashdall was curate of Orby - he recorded that he dined at Major Brackenbury's and stayed the night. He had a very bad headache but seemed to have enjoyed himself. At dinner were the Trollopes of Harrington and their niece, "a daughter of the authoress of 'Domestic Manners of the Americans'" - i.e. a sister of Anthony Trollope of the Barchester and Palliser novels. Also present were Alfred Tennyson, the Rawnsleys, the Cholmondeleys and Parker, the new Master of Hounds. Miss Trollope, aged 17, argued with some vivacity on Rashdall's side against Alfred Tennyson, then 23 years old. It sounds to have been an animated evening - no doubt the sherry was the strong sherry known as "the Consul's sherry", which John Macpherson used to send from Spain. Next morning, Rashdall breakfasted at Skendleby; he noted that they had family prayers. He added a note to his diary: "N.B. This house and its owner to be liked for the future much". Sadly he records no further visit to Skendleby, possibly because of the illness of Maria, wife of Major Brackenbury, who died the following July.

57.   Sir Edward worked with G.F. Heneage, who supported the Hunt with a subscription of L300, in finding a huntsman for the South Wolds in 1841, keeping the members of the Hunt on his side of the country informed. No doubt Surtees, who was fond of hunting tours, visited Skendleby to hunt with the South Wolds.

58.   Sir Edward was a magistrate and Deputy Lieutenant for Lincolnshire. In 1841, he was nominated for Sheriff, but declined the office. General Sir Henry Brackenbury, his nephew, remembered him well - "a fine commanding soldierly figure". He died in 1864.

59.   The fifth son of Richard of Aswardby died in infancy. The sixth son was William, born in 1789. He entered the Army and served in the 61st Regiment, as did his brother Edward. His father appears to have still been hard up in 1808, for in August of that year, when William was serving in Guernsey, he asked his father to purchase for him a lieutenancy in the 12th Regiment, saying that there was no other profession in which he could be so happy. Unfortunately the money could not be provided. In September, William wrote to his mother explaining the difficulties he was labouring under with only his pay to live on but he ends up "Never mind, I am happy and contented". Why could not his rich uncle in Raithby have helped?

60.   He went to the Peninsula in 1809 with the 1st Battalion of his Regiment. At the Battle of Talavera on 28 July that year, he was severely wounded, being shot between the shoulders. I think he must have been looked after by his brother Edward, because the Official History of the Regiment states that "on the advance of the enemy, the Spaniards abandoned Talavera and the wounded officers and soldiers fell into the hands of the French". William must have accompanied the Army in its retreat because it is certain that he was never a prisoner of the French. A year later he was back in England on his way to join the 2nd Battalion in Ireland. Then in 1811, he went back as a volunteer to Spain to the 1st Battalion. He was suffering a continual pain in his side from his wound, and a cough. He writes to his father on 2 July 1812: "I am tired enough of this country. Had I known that hard marching, bad living and no fighting would be my fate, I never would have left Ireland". He was soon enough to see fighting; on 23 July 1812 he was in the Battle of Salamanca, Wellington's masterpiece. He was again wounded - shot through the left foot and left cheek.

61.   Edward, who was then commanding one of Beresford's Portuguese regiments, wrote a letter from the battlefield to his parents: He had but a moment to write but wished his parents to receive his letter before they read of the battle in the papers. "The Almighty has been pleased once more in the midst of imminent danger to spare the life of both your sons". His brother William had been wounded but was under his care and there was no danger. "I must now in duty describe to you his wounds which he received when having grasped the Colours of the 61st Regiment within 25 yards of the French Column". He received the first ball through the left foot; the second ball he received in the left side of his face which broke the jawbone. "His noble and manly spirit surpasses anything I ever witnessed and he is patient to a degree beyond what I can describe, which is a great cause of his being quite free from fever, he thinks nothing of his sufferings. I dress his wounds for him and shall be able to remain with him some days longer".

62.   Edward goes on to describe and comment on the battle.
"I fought with my Portuguese Regiment who behaved well and bayonetted a Column of the French, you will scarcely believe how I could have escaped, when I assure you I was cutting away in a solid column with my common regulation sword but Providence protected me as it did at Badajoz when I mounted the Ladder at the head of my regt. Bill will write a post-script.." Then William writes that he was severely hit but was thankful that both he and his brother had been spared. "I have a volume to write you of Ned's unparalleled courage but I must wait until I get a little more strength".

63.   The wound in William's foot left him incurably lame and, I think, depressed and liable to self-pity. There is a sad letter to his father, written in February 1813. "I have suffered so much in these last three years (that is, since his first wound at Talavera) that I have learnt to consider illness as a matter of course". He wishes to be under the care of his London doctor but cannot afford to live in London. He would willingly return to Aswardby if he could afford to purchase a horse. "It may appear strange that I should require any other inducement to return home than the indulgence, comfort, kindness and affection which surround me at Aswardby. I assure you, father, I had rather be at home than any other place and were I able to walk, home would be everything to me. Had I a horse, my roving would be confined to a few miles around your own house". Why did his father not buy him a horse – or again, Robert Carr at Raithby? I suspect his father did not think his condition as bad as William's temperament made out. Perhaps Richard paid for him to stay on in London under the care of his doctor.

64.   Anyway, the following year he went off with his regiment to Newry. He writes more cheerfully of being with his old companions; he had no intention of volunteering for service in America. He met and fell in love with a Miss Atkinson, but as neither had any money marriage was out of the question. She married James T. Wallace, who came of a Northern Ireland family, and was in due course widowed. In 1820, William, by then retired on half-pay and a pension for wounds, married her. The marriage brought them both perfect happiness. When he died in 1844, his step-daughter wrote "He who was the idol of her young heart's affection, whose existence was entwined with her own, and who loved her with all the devotion and tenderness of his own faithful heart, is taken from her and she can only say "Thy Will be done."

65.   In 1837, William was living at Bolingbroke Hall where his youngest son was born. The next year he moved to Usselby Hall, where he was the tenant of Mr. Tennyson d'Eyncourt. In 1842, he had a stroke and was partly paralysed. The next year, he and his wife and younger children moved to Ahascreagh in Co. Galway, where they lived with his wife's sister and her husband. He died in June 1844, less than two months after his father had died at Aswardby.

66.   William had four sons and four daughters. The eldest son died unmarried at the age of 19. Three of the daughters also died young and unmarried. The second son, Richard Gunn Brackenbury, joined the 61st Regiment, which must have given pleasure to his father. After seeing service in the Indian Mutiny he died at Poona in 1859, unmarried.

67.   The third son, Charles Booth Brackenbury, joined the Royal Artillery and served in the Crimea. He became a Major-General and was Director of the Ordnance when he died in 1890. He was a cultivated man of great charm; a friend of Meredith and Ruskin. He wrote a military biography of Frederick the Great. The Dictionary of National Biography says of him: "Few men had seen so much of modern warfare on a large scale as General Charles Brackenbury and no one did more to spread sound ideas in England about the tactical changes demanded by the change in weapons". Two of his daughters were notable suffragettes; the portrait of Mrs. Pankhurst in the National Portrait Gallery is by one of them, who was an artist of some competence. His sons had a variety of careers, two becoming engineers, one a prosperous rancher in Denver, Colorado, and two went into the Indian Army. One died of typhoid contracted on the Bolan Pass in 1885, while the other was killed in the defense of the Residency in Manipur in 1891. On my death, the headship of the family will pass to a descendant of Charles Booth Brackenbury.

68.   The fourth son, Henry, was perhaps, after Robert Carr, the most distinguished of the descendants of Thomas of Steeping Magna. He was born in 1837 at Bolingbroke Hall. His early years were spent in youthful vagaries. It was not until he entered the Royal Military Academy at Woolwich in 1854 that he settled down to work. Helped by the influence of his uncle, Sir Edward, he was accepted for service in India during the Mutiny at the age of 20. There is a story that his commanding officer, in forwarding his application, would not support it on the grounds that he could not be spared as adjutant of the Royal Artillery in the Western District. When Sir Edward saw Sir Hew Ross, the Adjt. General of Artillery, the latter asked how old Henry was. "Only nineteen", said Sir Edward. "What, only nineteen, and his Colonel says he cannot be spared! He must be a good lad – he ought to have a chance on service". So his application was approved. He was invalided home in 1858. In 1873, he volunteered to serve in the Ashanti expedition in any capacity under General Sir Garnet Wolseley. This was the beginning of a fruitful connection, for Wolseley thought highly of him and took him on almost all his campaigns, including the campaign for the relief of Gordon. On returning home in August 1885 he was promoted Major-General. In 1886 he was appointed Head of the Intelligence Branch and served as such till 1891. He succeeded in revitalising the old department, collecting a vast amount of information which was published in a series of reports for the use of the War Office and other departments of Government. During the South African War of 1899, he was Director-General of Ordnance and his efficiency in improving the lamentable provision of munitions was generally acknowledged.

69.   Sir Henry was an able man with a considerable capacity for organization, with the determination to fight and fight again for what he wanted. He was a better soldier on the administrative and organizational side than a fighting soldier in the field. He is said to have been "an ugly man with a pasty face, a straggling moustache and a large, red nose". In common with many officers in stylish regiments he affected a lisp whereby all his "r"s were pronounced "w"s, "regiment" being pronounced "wegiment" and his own name "Bwackenbaywee". Wolseley, who hated camels, complained that the one given to him by the Khedive of Egypt made disgusting noises which reminded him of Brackenbury. On another occasion, Wolseley made a more complimentary comment when he said "Sir Henry Brackenbury is not one of the cleverest men in the Army – he is the cleverest man in the Army". When Sir Henry retired from the active list in 1904, he received a letter from Buckingham Palace from Lord Knollys. "His Majesty commands me to say that he sincerely appreciates the long, faithful and very valuable services which you have rendered to the Sovereign, the Army and the Country for so many years and in highly important posts, and he is anxious to mark his sense of them by conferring upon you, with the sanction of the Prime Minister, a Privy Councillorship". I do not know whether it was common for King Edward VII to make these awards himself rather than on the recommendation of the Prime Minister, but I have been told that this is the only case of a soldier receiving a Privy Councillorship on his retirement.

70.   Sir Henry was twice married but had no children. He died in 1914. I know little of his private life but I have seen a letter of his in which he says he is going down to spend two or three days with Anthony Trollope at Waltham, where he is to meet "Trevelyan the Competition Wallah".

71.   To return to Sir Edward and his descendants – his only child to live beyond 21 years was his son Edward Fenwick Brackenbury who served in the Chestnut Troop of the Royal Horse Artillery. He fought in the Zulu War. When he married he retired from the Army and eventually sold Skendleby. His wife was Emilie Marie, daughter of Major-General Shaw and elder sister of Flora Shaw, Lady Lugard. He had four sons and one daughter. He was an eccentric of great charm, irresponsible and a spend-thrift. When he died, my father had to cancel an order he had given to his shirtmaker for 365 shirts, one for every day in the year. He ran through a substantial fortune with the result that he was unable to give his children the start in life which they might have expected. Three of his sons qualified themselves as civil engineers. All four of them went to Africa to seek their fortunes. His daughter stayed to look after him and did not marry until after his death in 1907.

72.   His eldest son Edward was an inventor. He spent every penny which came his way on developing his inventions, but never achieved any success. In the late 1920s, he developed a method of "Jet Propulsion of Aircraft" but he was before his time and, although the Royal Society of Arts invited him to read a paper on the subject, no interest was shown by the aeronautics industry. When eventually jet aircraft were developed during the war, he had let his patents run out. I know nothing of aeronautics and cannot say whether his invention was a precursor of that used in the planes which eventually became so successful. Edward's son, Edward Lugard Brackenbury, made his career in the RAF. He died in 1981.

73.   The second son, Arthur, eventually became a District Officer in the Nyasaland Service where he was very happy. The third son, Harold, finding no success in Africa, signed on as a crew hand on a cargo ship in Cape Town. My mother told me that he used a false name and it was never possible to trace him thereafter. He was presumed lost at sea.

74.   My father was the youngest son, Reginald. He became a mining engineer and had an asbestos mine in the Transvaal but it failed. He then went into business in London. He married the elder daughter of Surgeon-General Sir William Taylor; her mother was a Thorndike and Sybil Thorndike her cousin. Reginald had two sons, Victor, the elder, and myself. My mother was Lady-in-Waiting to Princess Christian, daughter of Queen Victoria. The Princess was my brother's god-mother and asked that he should be called Victor after her son who had been killed in West Africa. My brother died in March, 1974, leaving an only daughter.

75.   While there are still many Brackenburys living in Lincolnshire, their connection with the family of which I have been speaking is difficult to find. The last close member of our family to live in Lincolnshire was Diana, who died last year. She was, I am sure, known to many of you, who will remember her integrity and loyalty. I recall what she wrote to me on her return from a journey, just after her eightieth birthday - she said "I am so happy to be back in my beloved Lincolnshire". I think that expresses the feelings of the family throughout the centuries for the county. Remember that Robert Carr and three of his four brothers, though brought up in Essex, all returned to Lincolnshire to make their lives there.

76.   That is all I have time to say of the Brackenbury family of Lincolnshire. The extravagance of my grandfather has resulted in his branch of the family leaving the county, something which I very much regret, because, in the last few years during which I have been coming here, I too have grown to love it.

77.   A postscript. My cousin, Mark Brackenbury, a descendant of General Charles Booth Brackenbury, is setting off from Woodbridge on this afternoon's tide to sail round the world in a 48ft ketch which he has had built to his own specifications. His wife, and his two children who are in their twenties, Claire and David, are accompanying him. They expect to be away for three years. We can wish them Godspeed and all success in their adventure.

As a rather fuller example of the activities of a Brackenbury in the thirteenth century may be cited the following:-

Robert of Brackenborough was juror of Louthesk Wapentake in 1298 and was listed as a member of assize there. In 1292, he appears in a list of those having Ь40 worth of land "who ought to be knights and are not" *(Chancery Miscellaneous 1/3, membrane 2)*. He is again, on 19 March 1298 listed as one of those having Ь40 worth of land (for the calling out of the feudal array to accompany the king in his campaign in Scotland) - *(Chancery Miscellaneous 1/6, membrane 30)*. His name however is also on the list of those doubtfully willing to take service with the king in Scotland. *(Ibid., membrane 32)*. I suspect that the government administration had let the first decision go by default and had not made Robert a knight even though he ought to have been; then having to find enough persons to complete the array for Scotland, they included his name on the grounds that as he had Ь40 worth of land he ought to be eligible. Robert demurred on the grounds that he should not be called upon for knight's service because he had never been made a knight, even though it was six years since it had been stated that he ought to be.

In November 1297, William Dyne of Burton impeded Robert de Brackenborough (i.e. obstructed his occupation) of 3 acres of meadow and 7 acres of woodland in Burton Coggles. William made fine of Ь10. *(Feet of Fines 1298)*. Again in May 1300, William Dyne impeded Robert, this time of 10 acres and 7 acres of meadow with appurtenances in Burton Coggles but made fine with him in Ь20. *(Feet of Fines 1300)*. In 1303, Robert held one fee in Brackenborough of the fees of John of Bayeux.

Burton Coggles is near Easton and Stoke Rochford and therefore a considerable distance from Brackenborough. There had already been difficulties for Robert in Burton Coggles. The Prior and chapter of Barnwell had presented Master Hugh of Hulme to the vacant living of Burton Coggles. Robert de Brackenborough claimed the right of presentation and put forward another candidate. The case was tried in the King's Court and a writ issued instructing the Bishop to accept the Prior's candidate. Hugh was therefore ordained subdeacon and installed at Hertford on 18 September 1288 and received letters patent.

SOME NOTES ON PANTON HALL

The Gace family figures in title deeds for Panton from 1688.
Carr Brackenbury the first married as his first wife Anne, daughter of
Langley Gace of Panton and Hardwicke in 1710. It was her brother who is
said to have built Panton in about 1720. It may well be that the Gaces
had built an earlier house at Panton.

In 1727, Joseph became Receiver for the estates of the Duke of
Kingston and by 1731 he owed the Duke £5,359, which he could not pay.
An Act of Parliament was passed in 1731-32 which enabled him to sell
part of his estates to settle his debt. In 1742, Carr Brackenbury the
second bought the mansion house and gardens and came to live in it.
He had just married his cousin, Isabella Booth. After Carr II's death,
his trustees sold Panton to Sir Jacob Wolff in 1767 and Wolff sold it to the
Turnors in 1773.

Panton has been attributed to Nicholas Hawksmoor but it has been
suggested that the architect was William Talman. In 1775, Turnor
employed John Carr of York to make extensive alterations to the house.
Hawksmoor's dates (1661 - 1736) would fit with a date of 1720 for Panton.
Talman on the other hand died in 1700 and therefore can only have built
at Panton for an earlier member of the Gace family. This is not
unlikely, for Talman had been employed by the Duke of Kingston on the
remodelling of Thoresby in Nottinghamshire in 1671. John Carr of York
also worked in the neighbourhood. He built the Town Hall in Newark and
rebuilt Thoresby in Nottinghamshire after Talman's house had burnt down.

Carr's house at Panton was demolished in the 1960s, but many of
its fittings were bought by Lord and Lady Iliffe and used in their
rescue operation at Basildon in Berkshire. Carr of York had worked at
Panton in 1775 and started at Basildon in 1776. The doors from Panton,
which fitted without alteration onto the hinges at Basildon, and the
chimneypiece in the dining room testify to the high quality of the work
at Panton. Panton must have been a much grander house than Basildon
- the facade had eleven bays to Basildon's seven - but it probably
lacked the particular grace of the latter, which is so suitable in the
soft charm of the Thames valley landscape. The grander style of Panton
would be better suited to its situation with a distant view of Lincoln
Cathedral. I have found no picture of the house as it was in Carr
Brackenbury's day but I have seen it stated that the gardens and walks
were laid out in the Dutch style, which at that time prevailed.

THE WILL AND CODICIL OF CARR BRACKENBURY, THE SECOND

Carr made his will in 1757 and added a codicil shortly before he died in 1763. At the time he made his will, he had six children, – Robert Carr, George, Edward, Anna Susanna, Elizabeth and Grace. He appointed three trustees, his brothers Joseph, Thomas and John Brackenbury, to whom he devised all his manors for 200 years in trust to raise Ⱡ10,000 to be paid to his children on their coming of age. At the time of his death, all his children were under age.

After he had made his will, he had four more children, William, Richard, Langley and Charlotte. He therefore by codicil charged the estate with a further sum viz. the greatest advance price that could be raised by selling his properties.

In neither his will, nor the codicil, did he appoint an executor. The codicil did not make clear the status of the four last children vis-à-vis those who benefited under the will. The trustees therefore brought a case in Chancery. The four last children, represented by their uncle Langley, (the brewer), were petitioners. The defendants were the six elder children, represented by the Trustees and Isabella, Carr's widow. The judge was asked to determine

    1. Who got what if the estate did not raise Ⱡ10,000?

    2. If more than Ⱡ10,000 was raised, did the petitioners have to share the excess with the defendants?

Two interesting points were made during the hearings. Isabella, the widow, declared herself provided for and claimed nothing but the coach and horses. Robert Carr stated that he inherited after his father's death from the entail set up by his grandfather.

The judge's decision was that the six elder children were entitled to Ⱡ10,000 before the other children got anything. Any further sums raised by the sale were to be divided between them all, share and share alike. As Panton was sold to Sir Jacob Wolff for Ⱡ5,600, it is unlikely that the estate reached much more than Ⱡ10,000.

LETTER FROM SALAMANCA

Salamanca, 24 July 1812.

My dearest Parents,

I have but a moment to write a few lines which I hope may be in time for the Post for England as should you see the papers before you receive this you will be naturally in a state of uneasiness. The Almighty has been pleased once more in the midst of the most Imminent danger to spare the life of both your sons. My dear brother William is wounded, but under my care; and with good surgical attendance is doing well: You will see by the papers he is severely wounded, but let me assure you my dear parents that there is no danger. I must now in duty describe to you his wounds, which he received when having grasped the Colours of the 61st Regt. within 25 yards of the French Column. He received the first ball through the Left foot, which passed through the bone, but as it has neither touched the ankle Joint, nor the Joints of his toes, his foot is safe, nor will he (I hope) be lame in consequence of it, although his cure may be tedious: the second ball he Received in the left side of his Face which broke the Jawbone; it is now setting; the wound is suppurating. He converses freely and takes nourishment without much pain. His noble and manly spirit surpasses anything I ever witnessed, and he is patient to a degree beyond what I can describe, which is a great cause of his being quite free of fever, he thinks nothing of his sufferings. I dress his wounds for him, and shall be able to remain with him some days longer.

So Glorious and Compleat a Victory has never been achieved by British Arms we had a general action in which the French were defeated, and worsted in every part, our army is following them up and whole Regts. of the Enemy throwing down their Arms and endeavouring vainly to escape: what their loss is I know not but a proclamation this morning stated it at fifteen thousand, Lord Wellington says 3,500 will cover our loss; we think the French cannot stand this side Madrid this is my idea also; but take care what we write never appears in Public. The 61st left 21* officers killed and wounded out of 26 who entered the action, the remaining Five with 75 men only gained the Hill they were destined to take and destroy the enemy. I fought with my Portuguese Regt. who behaved well and bayonetted a Column of the French, you will scarcely believe how I could have escaped, when I assure you I was cutting away in a Solid Column with my Common regulation Sword: but Providence protected me as it did at Badajos, when I mounted the Ladder at the Head of my Regt. Bill will write a postscript, believe me my dearest Parents your ever dutifull son,

Edwd. Brackenbury.

*N.B. The "Gazette" announces 24. J.M.B.

My dear Parents, by the description my brother had given you of my Wounds, you will perceive I am severely hit, but God has been graciously pleased to spare us both and I am thankfull I have a Volume to write you of Ned's unparallelled courage, but I must wait until I get a little more Strength. I will thank you to write on receipt of this to my Brother John – to my sister Jemima, and to my Uncle William. I remain my dearest Parents yours by every tie of Affection.

William Brackenbury
Lt. 61st Regt.

Printed by Advance Publicity Service, 8 West Parade, Lincoln. Telephone : 25066